A Disappearing
WORLD

Rob Waring, *Series Editor*

T0052131

HEINLE
CENGAGE Learning

Australia • Brazil • Japan • Korea • Mexico • Singapore • Spain • United Kingdom • United States

Words to Know

This story is set in Africa. It happens in the countries of Congo [kɒŋgoʊ] and Gabon [gæboʊn], in an area called the Congo Basin.

 A **An Expedition.** Read the paragraph. Then match each word with the correct definition.

   This story is about an expedition that travels through parts of Congo and Gabon. The trip starts just north of the equator. The leader of the trip, Michael Fay, is with the Wildlife Conservation Society. His team's aim is to document the wildlife of this beautiful and completely natural part of the world. They must do it before this natural beauty disappears and is gone forever. The biggest challenge for the group will be to cross the varied, and sometimes dangerous, landscape of the Congo Basin.

1. expedition _____

2. the equator _____

3. conservation _____

4. wildlife _____

5. disappear _____

6. challenge _____

7. landscape _____

a. animals and plants that live in natural conditions

b. an imaginary line around Earth's middle

c. a difficult task that tests one's skill or will

d. the features of a land area

e. the protection of plants, animals, or natural areas

f. a journey organized for a special purpose

g. go away suddenly and not return

B **Wildlife in a Wild Land.** Here are some land formations on the expedition. Write the correct word next to each formation.

hills	ocean	rain forest	rapids

4. _____

1. _____

2. _____

An Expedition

3. _____

Distances
1 kilometer = .62 miles
1 meter = 3.3 feet

It's September in the Congo. Here, just north of the equator, an expedition unlike any other is about to begin. A team of scientists and researchers will travel for almost 2,000 kilometers through a rain forest in the middle of Africa. However, this isn't just any rain forest. This one covers over 150,000 **square kilometers!**[1]

There has never been an expedition quite like this before. The aim of the expedition is to make a scientific record of the unusual and special world of the Congo Basin; a world which could be disappearing from Earth.

---

[1]**square kilometer:** the area of a square with sides of one kilometer

 CD 1, Track 07

Dr. Michael Fay is a scientist from the Wildlife Conservation Society. He is leading the group. He calls the expedition 'The Megatransect,' or 'the big crossing.' The expedition will go all the way across the Congo Basin. He and his team will travel around 2,000 kilometers through the rain forests of Congo and Gabon.

The conservation of this rain forest is very important to Fay. He feels the area is a very special place that's disappearing. He says that if they don't document the wildlife here now, there may never be another chance to do it. Fay explains in his own words: "What I'm trying to do, in a **desperate**[2] way, is to show the world that we're just about to lose the last little **gem**[3] in the African **continent**.[4] And if we don't do something now...if we don't do it today, we can forget about it."

---

[2]**desperate:** having an immediate, very strong need
[3]**gem:** a jewel; a very valuable thing
[4]**continent:** one of the main land areas of Earth

Infer Meaning

1. Why does Michael Fay feel 'desperate'?

2. What does Fay mean when he says
   "we can forget about it"?

The Congo Basin is one of the world's most important natural areas. It contains almost one quarter of the world's rain forests. It may also have up to half of all of the wild plants and animals found in all of Africa.

Fay's plan is to collect and record data on almost every part of the rain forest. He plans to do this by walking all the way through the forest. During this time, he wants to document the trees, the plants, and the animals that he sees there. It's a big job, and it's going to take a very long time.

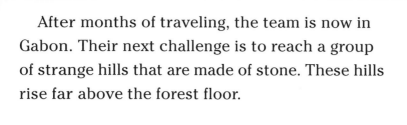

After months of traveling, the team is now in Gabon. Their next challenge is to reach a group of strange hills that are made of stone. These hills rise far above the forest floor.

The men reach the base of the hills. They slowly begin to walk up. Then, suddenly, they realize that they are finally above the tops of the trees. They have a wonderful view of everything around them!

From the top of the hills, the team can see very far in every direction.

Fay describes what the team can see. "We can see a long way here, you know…70 or 80 kilometers in every direction. We can see **360 degrees**[5] around."

In today's world, it's unusual to be in a place where there are no other people. Fay also points this out. "There are no humans," he says. "There's not a single **village**,[6] there's not a single road." This makes it clear just how special and completely natural this African rain forest really is. "It's an **amazing**[7] place," he adds.

---

[5]**360 degrees:** a complete circle
[6]**village:** a group of houses that is a lot smaller than a town
[7]**amazing:** surprising; wonderful

The team continues on their long trip. As they go, they can hear their next challenge before they reach it. Rapids!

"Okay, wow," says Fay when he sees them—The **Kongou Chutes**.[8] These rapids are an important part of the landscape that the team wants to protect. This area is a land of fast-moving water and very old forests. Both of these things are currently in danger because of **logging**.[9] Businesses want to come here. They plan to cut down the trees so they can sell them as wood. If this happens, it will be very bad for the animals and plants in the area. It will also be bad for the land itself.

But, right now, the team has a more immediate problem. These rapids are very fast and very dangerous! According to Fay's plan, the team must cross the river here. Will they be able to cross safely? If they do, how will they do it?

---

[8]**Kongou Chutes:** [kɒŋgu ʃuts]
[9]**logging:** the work or industry of cutting trees

Predict

Answer the questions. Then scan page 16 to check your answers.

1. How will the team cross the dangerous rapids?

2. What will they need to do it?

The crossing is only a few hundred meters wide, but getting across it is not an easy task. The team members have a lot of experience. They use **guide ropes**,[10] **stepping stones**,[11] and everything they know to get across the dangerous waters safely.

After a lot of hard work, everyone finally makes it across the rapids. However, the team has to spend a lot of time doing it. It takes them a full day to get themselves and their supplies across the rapids, and they still have a very long way to go!

---

[10] **guide rope:** a thick cord that people follow to find a way
[11] **stepping stone:** small stones, usually in water, that people walk on

stepping stones

guide rope

After more than a year, the team finally reaches the end of their travels. They are at the Atlantic Ocean at last, and they are all very pleased to be there. Later, Fay describes how he felt as he took those final steps through the rain forest. "We'd been walking in the woods in our own little world for fifteen months and now it was over," he says. "I was **overwhelmed**."[12]

In the end, Dr. Michael Fay and his team walked around 2,000 kilometers through some of the wildest lands of Africa. Along the way, they documented as many of the things they found as possible. They did it all as part of the challenging scientific expedition called 'The Megatransect.' They also did it in an attempt to save a disappearing world.

---

[12] **overwhelmed:** having a very strong feeling

After You Read

1. Compared to other rain forests, the Congo Basin is:
   A. small
   B. average size
   C. dark
   D. large

2. What is the main purpose of the expedition?
   A. to study and record information
   B. to walk a long way
   C. to disappear
   D. to meet people

3. In paragraph 2 on page 6, the word 'we' refers to:
   A. the Wildlife Conservation Society
   B. the people of the world
   C. scientists
   D. the Megatransect

4. Dr. Michael Fay thinks the Congo Basin is:
   A. safe
   B. fortunate
   C. in trouble
   D. forgettable

5. In paragraph 1 on page 8, the word 'contains' can be replaced by:
   A. collects
   B. has
   C. records
   D. takes

6. The Congo Basin has _____ of the plants found in Africa.
   A. all
   B. a few
   C. none
   D. many

7. Which will Dr. Fay probably NOT document during his trip?
  A. trees
  B. people
  C. animals
  D. plants

8. Which is a good heading for page 10?
  A. A View of Everything
  B. No Animals, No Village
  C. Team Can See a Short Way
  D. Low Stone Hills

9. In paragraph 1 on page 13, the word 'describes' can be replaced by:
  A. asks
  B. tells about
  C. wonders
  D. believes

10. Who is 'they' in the phrase 'they plan to cut' on page 14?
  A. the expedition
  B. the animals
  C. logging businesses
  D. the Kongou Chutes

11. What does the team use to cross the rapids?
  A. stepping stones
  B. guide ropes
  C. experience
  D. all of the above

12. Crossing the Kongou Chutes is a _____ task.
  A. slow
  B. simple
  C. quick
  D. safe

The Wildlife Conservation Society
WHAT IS IT?

The goal of the Wildlife Conservation Society (WCS) is to protect a wide range of animals. Some of the world's animals are endangered, or currently in danger of disappearing from the earth. The WCS is also involved in the protection of animal environments. Saving these natural areas of land will allow certain animals to live and increase in number. The challenge of this work is becoming increasingly difficult. Humans are taking over more of the places where animals used to live.

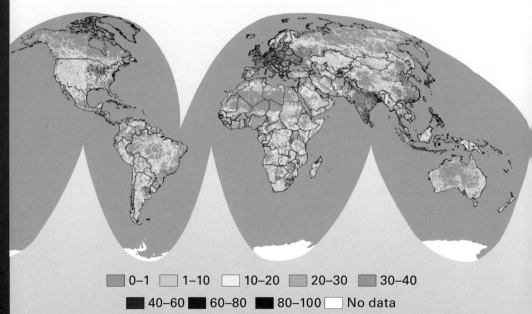

☐ 0–1 ☐ 1–10 ☐ 10–20 ☐ 20–30 ☐ 30–40
☐ 40–60 ☐ 60–80 ☐ 80–100 ☐ No data
1 = very little influence   100 = heavy influence

Human Influence on Earth

Source: World Wildlife Fund/U.S. Conservation Science Program

The WCS works in four major areas:

SCIENCE

Over a hundred years ago, the WCS added its first animal specialist, Dr. Reid Blair, to its staff. Since then, the WCS Wildlife Health Sciences Division has become a world leader in this field. Today, these study and research activities help care for more than 17,000 animals in parks in the United States and around the world.

INTERNATIONAL CONSERVATION

Humans now live on most parts of the earth. People must carefully consider how to best use the few untouched areas that remain. They must also give special consideration to endangered animals. The WCS land conservation program concentrates on these areas.

EDUCATION

The 'Living Landscapes' program is just one way the WCS helps to protect endangered animals. It provides parks where endangered animals can live safely, which is an important first step. However, animals don't know

"Humans are taking over more of the places where animals used to live."

where these parks end. Therefore, local people must also learn how to treat the animals outside of the park area. Therefore, the Living Landscapes Program helps to educate local communities.

CITY WILDLIFE PARKS

Since 1895, the main WCS office has been in the largest park in New York. School children visit city parks every day of the week to learn about conservation. Several programs are available in the park system, including family events, discovery centers where people can experience the wildlife, and wildlife theaters.

CD 1, Track 08

Word Count: 315
Time: _____

Vocabulary List

360 degrees (13)

amazing (13)

challenge (2, 10, 14, 19)

conservation (2, 6)

continent (6)

desperate (6, 7, 19)

disappear (2, 4, 6, 19)

equator (2, 4)

expedition (2, 3, 4, 6, 19)

gem (6)

guide rope (16, 17)

hill (3, 10, 11)

landscape (2, 14)

logging (14)

ocean (3, 19)

overwhelm (19)

rain forest (3, 4, 6, 8, 10, 13, 19)

rapids (3, 14, 15, 16)

square kilometer (4)

stepping stones (16)

village (13)

wildlife (2, 3, 6, 19)